My Complete 180

3 Simple Strategies to Shift Your Mindset &
Transform Your Life

Written by A. Marie Davis

Editor: Jessica LeeAnn

Book Design & Cover: Danny Media

www.chocolatereadings.com

Dedicated to my daughters Cheyenne and Nyesa.

Prologue

It's been said that hindsight is 20/20. I say hindsight is only 20/20 when you look back and actually see clearly. I have had so many road sign moments in my life. Road signs yelling and shouting at me such as, "Do Not Enter," "Wrong Way," "Make a U-Turn," yet I still kept going.

We've all seen signs like these in our lives. For some of us, we've experienced these more frequently than others. I heard loud and clear that I was going down the wrong path, yet I kept pushing along just like the ice cream man on a hot Saturday afternoon.

Why do we do this to ourselves?

At some point in time, everyone has heard that little voice or had that gut feeling that tells us something isn't quite right or what we're doing is absolutely wrong. It then becomes a question of what do you do about it?

If I had one solid answer for that, I'd win the Nobel Peace prize! I do have a theory, though. I believe it has a lot to do with the fact that these moments have to be a part of our life story in order to make us who we must become.

There are a lot of things that have happened to me, and at the time I couldn't understand why.

Now, looking back at them, I see these moments have prepared me for the next levels of my life. Each moment in my life has led to a 180, a shift, a transformation.

I made a 180 on my journey, and you can, too! You're thinking, why not a 360? Making a 360 will only lead you to where you were in the first place, and that is the last thing you want to do!

Allow me to take you through the journey that catapulted my 180. The experience I went through felt like a dark hole with no end in sight. This was because I was doing a 360 with my life. I was ignoring the road signs. Road signs being warnings from family and friends, snide remarks and rude comments spewed at me during my weakest moments, and the physical torment repeatedly thrashed upon my body and ego. I did not see any pattern of revelation happening. I often asked myself why my life like this was. Where did I take a wrong turn?

Strange as it may sound, these moments are strategically mapped out. These types of situations happen in order to get us on the right path. Sometimes we don't always catch the hint, but no matter how many times you make decisions that send your world into a tailspin, it's all about what we do with the outcome that makes all the difference.

Get Ready

The 180 experience will take you through the highs and lows I went through in order to transform my life. In the end, it will all be worth it when you can look back and see all of the unnecessary baggage you can leave behind. You'll learn the three steps that I took towards my journey to freedom: Admit, Assess, & Address.

Taking these three steps allowed me to grow. If you desire to grow, you'll need physical, mental, and emotional willpower to get through the hurdles, struggles, and mountains that may stand in your way. You have to dig yourself out from the deepest hole, even if the effort it entails doesn't seem worth it. Trust me, it's really worth it!

It takes emotional, mental, and physical strength to get to a place of peace and acceptance. We must choose to individually get to that place. It won't happen on its own. It is going to take hard work and dedication to arrive at this place. Everyone has the ability to make a 180. However, not everyone is willing. Are you?

Admit

Admitting that there are things that you need to refine about yourself before entering into new relationships is paramount. From a young girl, I was never encouraged to love myself. I had no strong sense of self. I witnessed a number of abusive and unhealthy relationships. There were many devastating experiences in my life that tore me apart at times. This all played an intricate part in the types of relationships I found myself in – starting with my ex-husband.

Mr. Wrong

I married young in 2001. I was twenty-six years old when I got married. I already had a four year old daughter from a previous relationship. I thought getting married was the "right" thing to do at the time. I also felt like if someone wanted to marry ME, I needed to jump on it. This was a prime example of my low self-esteem being at the forefront of my decision making. The marriage didn't go as either of us planned, and I wanted out! Five years was all I could tolerate. There were rumors of him cheating. I painfully found out he had a sex addiction, and I didn't see any way that I could help him or love him through that. So in November of 2006, I took my two children, attached them and the bags to my hip, and walked out on my husband.

It took years for us to get divorced. My ex-husband never wanted to sign the papers. So for nine years we were legally married, and yet very much legally separated. Since we weren't living together anymore, I began a new relationship sometime in January of 2007.

My husband and I were very connected to our church. And once I told him about the new relationship, he made sure the entire church knew as well. It was embarrassing and painful for me.

Although unethical, my "adulterous" affair helped soothe the stress and unloving imprisonment my marriage unkindly bestowed upon me. Jumping into that relationship when I was still so wounded from ending my marriage, plus the fact that I already had a sense of worthlessness, encouraged me to make decisions that would deepen the wounds I already carried before I knew a 180 was needed.

Admitting My Truth

What I learned from the experience with my ex-husband was that my own mindset contributed to the demise of my marriage. In order for me to grow, I had to admit my way of acting and thinking at that time in my life had to change. The reluctance to admit I needed inner change led me into the departure of my marriage and the arrival of my adulterous affair.

Because the truth can be hard to embrace, we tend to stay away from it. However, admitting to the truth brings about a sense of ownership. It means you are taking responsibility of the changes you need to make.

At the time of my affair, I couldn't admit that I was wrong, even though I knew it from the beginning. The light in my eyes blocked the warning signs posted in my conscious. It could have been the eyelids I had shut over the reality of my life, but whatever it was, I ignored all precautionary signs and began a relationship that could have ended me.

Prince Not So Charming

My low self-esteem and wounded heart caused me to pursue the new relationship in the beginning. I owned a salon/spa at the time in Brooklyn, NY. An event I was planning in my salon kept me there a lot of late nights. As I was shutting down the gate one night, a slight click of a car door lock made me look his way.

He looked, too.

I looked some more. Our constant gaze left me paralyzed as he got into his BMW and drove off. 32 years old and I was as flighty as a school girl! I was still looking for Prince Charming. And I think I may have found him.

To some, I would be considered brave for the move I was about to make, but to others they would shout "Hey Anneka, there goes your warning sign!" but I made my move anyway. The next evening, I walked across the street to the police station that stood across from my salon. My hands lifted the wiper blade gingerly off the glass of his BMW series. A surgeon couldn't have had sturdier hands the way I placed an invitation on his window and replaced the blade back in position to stop it from flying away. I made sure the statement 'read me' shone boldly on top of the blade, then I walked away.

The next day I received a phone call. The deep, sensual voice on the other end of the phone confirmed he read the invitation. He told me he had a shift the night of the event, but would stop by before he starts work at the police station. He was a cop!

Of course your girl was dressed to kill! With a pink, low cut dress reaching just above the knees, and a pair of 6-inch black stilettos, you couldn't tell your girl nothing! I was going to make sure he would notice me and want me.

He showed up and he brought a friend, too. From my peripheral, I could see him and his friend checking me out. Confirming my goods.

In front of my face, they had an open conversation about the fact that I was actually pretty. They talked about my cute toes, my cleavage, and whatever else they mumbled and chuckled to each other.

My diva spirit was flattered. My conscious; not so much. My spirit said this was all wrong. They were sizing me up like I was a piece of meat at the butcher. Right then and there I should have admitted that I was being desperate. I was faking that I was a self-assured woman. I should have admitted that jumping into another relationship was only going to bring me more turmoil. I should have admitted that I didn't need Prince Charming. What I needed was to take stock of my life, by myself and engage in my own self display so I could start making my 180.

I didn't admit any of it. So after I was put on display like a show dog, they left and he promised to call me.

He did.

Alarm, Alarm

Answering that call opened up the door of a three year long battle that turned into physical, emotional, financial and mental abuse.

We were dating for four months before I noticed his jealous and controlling demeanor. An argument over a trip to Atlantic City revealed his true colors. I will never forget the manipulation and emotional damage he caused that led to my path of deeper destruction with him. I couldn't believe I had let it get so deep!

The choice to submit to his abuse left me homeless. I lost my business, and was temporarily without one of my children. Yes, I use the word choice, because we all have the power of choice.

My oldest daughter, who was twelve years old at the time, made the choice to live with her biological father because she couldn't tolerate seeing me in an abusive relationship anymore. The idea of my daughter leaving me was not an easy pill to swallow. My youngest daughter cried for her sister constantly. She persistently asked where she was and why she wasn't home. Those types of questions made it that much harder to accept her absence.

Five Steps

When my daughter left, I felt like my heart was ripped from my chest. With her absence, I found myself in a stage of anger for a long time. I felt like I may have gone through the Kubler-Ross model five stages of grief over her departure.

The five stages of grief can be applied to any type of loss. The five steps are: *Denial, Anger, Bargaining, Depression*, and *Acceptance*. Not everyone experiences each step, and not everyone's grief goes in the same sequence. For example: someone can be angry before they are in denial. Others may go straight to acceptance. The stages are individual and specific to each person. Let's break them all down.

Denial is when you can't or don't want to believe what's happening. It could be a death, a divorce, even seeing a child go off to college. It doesn't seem real and it becomes hard to conceive. It becomes a coping mechanism to avoid, even believe, what is going on.

Anger seems self-explanatory, but it isn't always as simple as being mad. Anger can be hostile, but also used as protection. Anger can be a catalyst for change. It can motivate you to do things differently.

Bargaining is like any other negotiation. You want to make the loss disappear somehow. You want to convince the pain to go away. You want to feel like you're in control over something you have no control over at all.

Depression - We tend to mistake sadness for depression. Depression used here describes living the reality that you have suffered a loss in either a person or situation and it could cause you to withdraw.

Acceptance is where you get to the point that what is real is really real. It doesn't have to mean that things have to stay the way they are.

As a Social Worker, I understood this process; I realized that I was buried in anger, hurt and disappointment. The only way I could dig myself out was to admit I no longer wanted to be angry. I no longer wanted to be separated from my daughter.

I had to forgive myself. I had to forgive her. I knew it was not going to be easy to restore our relationship. I had to let go of that angry place that comforted and protected me for so long.

It was about ten months before my oldest daughter and I had face to face contact.

The Shift

At the first sign of abuse, I should have done what the old country song says, "These boots were made for walking," and I should have used mine to walk all over him and right out of the door.

I didn't.

So my choice reaped deep and painful consequences. I also reaped the 180 that I so desperately needed in my life at the time. That revelation did not come until I was on my bathroom floor, contemplating slitting my wrists with broken glass and swallowing about seventy extra strength Tylenol pills.

I just wanted out at that moment. I wanted to rid myself of all the pain and somehow cleanse myself of the weakness that I couldn't constructively address. I was crying my eyeballs out. Then I heard that voice. The one you hear deep in the pit of your gut. Yeah, that voice.

God!

I was on that bathroom floor, and it was like He said "Girl get your butt up off that floor!"

I slowly picked my broken self, up off of that cold, needed to be mopped--I thought I swept all the hair up--white tiled floor, and started to dry the river of tears off of my face. Sitting quietly on my baron living room floor I asked God how I was supposed to go about putting all the broken pieces of my crumbled life back together?

His answer was that I needed to start over. I needed to let go of the notion that I needed to put together all the pieces. Instead I needed to figure out which of these pieces was worth keeping. I kept those that were necessary for me to begin the 180 journey.

I was ready to confess to myself what was really going on in my life and truly own it!

Make That Change

The act of change I believe is one of the scariest concepts for humans. Change is so difficult because we are afraid of the unknown. The possibility that we could be happy, successful, and have the power to create the life we truly desire, scares the hell out of us. As does the fear of failure.

We really do have the power and ability to control our destiny. It is all about making a decision, even if you're not ready. Start by admitting, then you can move and start assessing; which will lead to creating your plan of action.

God showed me three steps that I needed to take in order to start my 180, and I want to share those steps with you. Ready?

Admitting

The first step is to take the ownership that there is something not quite right in your life and you need to make changes. This step is all about transformation. You're walking away from where you are; the place that is holding you back from your future, the place that is holding you back from your freedom. It is important you go through each step carefully. You can think of it as a secret confession to yourself. If you are more of the brave type, shout it to the world! Either way, be honest with yourself.

For me it was admitting I was in a manipulative and abusive relationship. I also needed to do something about my poor self-image. I had to own up to my role in the chaos I created in my life.

During the Admitting phase, I'd suggest getting a journal. Take it with you wherever you go. If you prefer to journal on your phone, tablet, IPad or computer, that's fine, too. The purpose is to organize your ideas, emotions, and truths about yourself. You're not discussing anything with anyone but you. You MUST be honest. The true transformation will not occur unless you journal honest, true, real insight about yourself. Dig deep. Even if it hurts to admit suppressed things about yourself, you will find healing if you work your 180 as described.

Admitting equals removing the superficial. It's a positive way to remove all of the layers and reveal your true self to you. You do not have to share your deep diving self-expedition if you're not comfortable. However, if you believe others in your circle could benefit, simply buy them this book.

Admitting I needed to change was my first wake up call to my 180. I had all the revelations about myself, but didn't know what to do with it.

That bathroom floor and all of the feelings that were derived from that experience will always be the turning point in my life. That is where I could see there was a transformation coming. I knew my life needed and deserved that change more than anything.

Admitting that there needs to be a change in your life, means being honest with yourself. Being honest with yourself, means stripping your soul naked, digging deep down to your core, and being willing to see through the surface.

You must remove the layers that we all sometimes hide behind. One of my layers was hiding the fact that I was in an abusive relationship that left me and my six year old daughter living in my car for months. If that's not a wakeup call, I don't know what is.

We portray the personification that everything is well with our soul, and that we have it all together. We hide behind layers of guilt, shame, embarrassment, insecurity, jealousy, people pleasing, being vulnerable, inadequacy, entitlement or the lack thereof.

Often times, these layers are the things that prevent us from living an authentic life. We also allow others to define us and sometimes even create who we are or who we should be.

After I got up from the bathroom floor, I began to take the first step in changing my life. It began with me admitting that I was not where I wanted and needed to be in life.

Admitting is as intricate as peeling an onion. You want to peel layer by layer until you get to the core. Admitting is your doorway to freedom and the road to obtaining a new life. Making a 180 releases you from the bondage that holds you down. There are some steps you must take while doing this.

The first step of the journey to your 180 is to not only admit the problem, but confess the things you need to change. There are things that we all can improve upon in our lives, like our personal relationships, communication, financial life and attitudes toward life in general.

Surviving an abusive relationship caused me to learn how to define my life, and re-create the woman I needed to be on my own terms.

Now, your situation does not have to be as traumatic as my experience to promote change. However, chaos and crisis are usually the catalyst for change.

My chaos and crisis was myself. I allowed myself to get involved with someone who would ultimately cost me everything - my self-esteem, my family, my money, my business, my children, and ultimately myself. What or who is your chaos?

If you are at a point in your life where you are ready to step away and remove the mask and strip away the layers to reveal your true self, just know it can be done, but there is real work involved. You have to admit to yourself that you need to make some changes. How do you do that?

In order to define your true self, admit that you just want to be YOU, but you may have to find out who that is first.

How I Got Here

In 2010, I hit rock bottom. That's when I had to come to the realization that the abuse, losing my home and business coupled with the severed relationship between me and my oldest daughter--adding the strong urge to end my life-- were all on me. Yes, they were all on me, but it wasn't all my fault. The bulk of my problems were a result of my own negative thinking and low self-esteem. I had no real grasp or understanding of my self-worth. I didn't know that I deserved better. I should have demanded nothing less than greatness in my life.

It took a while, but I finally realized the relationship that I was in was going to kill me. I had to come up with a way to remove myself from it. In the beginning I must admit, I was like a mad scientist using my formulas and techniques on myself before I came up with the perfect antidote. You can relax in knowing the steps I share with you are tried and true with positive results.

Questions for Thought

What is the one thing you have to admit to yourself?

_____

_____

_____

_____

_____

Why do you feel you're ready to act now?

_____

_____

_____

_____

_____

Who are you really making the change for?

_____

_____

_____

_____

_____

How has your current situation affected you? Your finances? Other relationships? Your school/work?

_____
_____
_____
_____
_____
_____
_____

How will you sustain the changes you plan to make?

_____
_____
_____
_____
_____

What do you think prompted you make the choices you made to be in your current situation?

_____
_____
_____
_____
_____

What does your future look like to you?

_____

_____

_____

_____

_____

_____

_____

_____

_____

_____

_____

_____

_____

_____

_____

_____

_____

_____

_____

_____

_____

_____

_____

_____

PART 2

Assess

Often times we are defined by either what we do or who we are in people's lives. We are someone's parent, spouse, boss, friend, child or employee.

I spent most of my life believing that I was worth nothing, and would receive nothing. I had thoughts that were beneath what God really had in store for me. I was so desperate to be loved and accepted. I had no real sense of identity.

Creating my own 180 Experience has been challenging, and at times still is. In some areas, it is a daily task. I have worked hard to train my thoughts to never retreat back to the places that held me in darkness.

In 2010, I was in the recovery process of escaping the abusive relationship I was in. Since I had lost everything that meant anything to me, I started from the bottom and began to put my life back together, piece by piece. The first piece of my life I focused on putting back together was the relationship with my daughter.

In the early times of my oldest daughter being separated from me, she made numerous attempts to speak with me. She texted me, emailed me, used other family members to get a message to me. I was being a stubborn mule for ten months and ignored all of her requests and attempts. I was so wounded by her decision to live away from me.

Losing my relationship with my oldest daughter was by far the most devastating experience for me. She made the choice to live with her father, a man she barely knew. I see now that she was just desperate to find a way to snap me out of that cloud of darkness I was living in.

My oldest daughter's father was not very active in her life prior to her choosing to live with him. He had made up his mind when I chose to leave him that if he couldn't have me he didn't want any involvement in our daughter's life. The tears that flowed from my eyes quickly dried up from the rage my heart was pumping behind the thought of his threat. The threat which actually turned into a promise since he followed through on it.

My daughter unwittingly gave this man the ammunition to damage my whole being while he plotted and then used the information against me in court. Many years before, he found out I was getting married so he sued me to get custody of her. It turned into a twelve year battle.

To say I avoided my daughter would be putting it lightly. Her decision to live with her father at that time, made him think he won. My circumstances during that time were:

- I was homeless and living in my car,
- My income was low (shamefully around $22,000 while raising a toddler), and

- I was in an abusive relationship.

These things were the leverage he needed to gain temporary custody of her. The traitor (I had better words for her at the time) used the impact of the abusive relationship as her excuse to abandon ship.

After twelve years of raising her on my own as a single parent without child support from the other parent, she had the nerve to leave me in my most desperate time. A daughter is supposed to stick with her mother through everything, so I thought. She is supposed to let her mother know when the guy is not right for her, so I thought. A daughter should take her mother with her and protect her when she sees her mother in danger, so I thought. As much as I thought of what a mother-daughter relationship was supposed to be, we obviously didn't have that. We had betrayal, hurt, anger, and deception. I put too much responsibility on her. This was not her role. I needed to end the abuse.

A huge part of my heart died the day she left. Over the years there were so many pieces of my heart that fell off and died, I began to feel I would die heartless.

How I Assessed
After ten long months had gone by of me being stubborn and my daughter doing anything to get a

hold of me, I finally gave into what I knew I wanted all along, and that was to have my daughter in my life again.

It was via a response to an email she sent me that rekindled our familial flame. Initially I was annoyed at the content of her email, but then I realized that what she was trying to do was capture my attention any way she could. I decided to respond, one by disciplining her about the content, (hey, I'm still her mother). Then I proceeded to offer her a time and place for us to sit down face-to-face and talk. This was going to be a challenge because her father didn't want us seeing each other. However, once I made the decision to break this cycle of emptiness between us, I didn't care about how he felt or what he would have to say.

I took her to lunch after school one afternoon. We went to our favorite Colombian restaurant. We talked about the fact that I was no longer in the abusive relationship, and how that felt for both of us. I remember promising her sometime before she left that I was going to end it, but I just needed time because I needed a plan. At the time, she couldn't receive or understand that. She thought it was just as simple as walking out the door and it would all be over. While we were reconnecting, I explained that to her. She did seem to have a better understanding. She apologized for leaving, and I apologized for everything. I also wanted to make sure she understood that in the end I loved her, would do anything for her, but she needed to respect that I was the adult and although in disagreement with some of my decision making, I did not see it as a reason for her to make such an adult-like decision, with long term consequences.

During the duration of her living with her father, she had the misfortune of learning what a horrible person and awful father he was. It was a harsh lesson for her to learn. After a year with him, she ran away from his home and came to me. He actually called the cops, because he too was a cop (what was it with me and cops?) to come and get my daughter from me. It was just another way for him to try and punish me because he still hated me for leaving. Once we got to the police station, he actually had the audacity to approach me, reaching out to me, asking if we could talk. I was so steaming mad, and I aggressively rejected his request. That only heightened his anger, but at the time I didn't care because I couldn't believe that his disdain for me superseded his love and protection for his child. Who wants to see their daughter in the back of a police car and brought to a police station all because he wants to punish the mother of his child because he can't have her?

After this fiasco, my daughter begged me to file a petition with the courts to regain custody of her. So after having some deep introspection, a conversation with her about her behavior, respect, and us working together to rebuild our relationship, I did just that.

The New York State Court system is flawed to say the least. I waited months for a court date and endured emotional beatings every court appearance until finally, my daughter and her father got into an altercation leading up to the cops being called. Her father put her out and told her he never wanted to see her again. I was sad for this moment and every other moment her father neglected her, but glad that I could have my baby back again without the fighting.

I took time to nurture our relationship back to health by finding outside support systems for us corporately and her individually. We spent a lot of time together talking, listening, going out together, having photo shoots, me teaching her to drive, planning her sweet sixteen and preparing her for college. She is now about to be a college graduate and it feels so good to know that we have mended our relationship in spite of my abusive relationship and her father's lack of involvement.

The Escape

The three years I had remained in the abusive relationship; I felt trapped. In many ways I felt as though I deserved to be treated the way he had treated me. I felt hopeless and I was deeply depressed. I desperately wanted to get out of the abusive relationship that had caused so much damage, but I didn't have the resources or support to make that happen. When I did begin to come out of isolation to seek help and told friends and family about my current status, no one came to my rescue or wanted to help. It had finally come down to my oldest sister who was just getting her life together after living many years on the streets, addicted to drugs. However, she was the only one willing to help me and my youngest daughter.

One night my abuser tried to choke me to death. My immediate strategy was survival. My youngest daughter laid asleep on his couch while he attempted to end my life on his basement floor. Prior to the basement incident, my abuser demanded I remove all of my clothing so that he could have sex with me. Since I didn't comply, he poured a bottle of cold water all over me.

I didn't have a place to stay, but I knew I needed to flee his prison. I ran to his basement in an attempt to gather some clothing for my daughter and I. Everything else I owned as far as furniture or other material goods were stored in his garage. Since his garage was inadequately sealed, all elements seeped in (especially rain) and destroyed my possessions anyway so there was no need to even think of wanting them.

41

The basement obviously wasn't a safe haven. The sound of an avalanche followed a few minutes after. He was right behind me. I thought my ankles broke as he pulled me off the bed I was sitting on, and he proceeded to choke me. It wasn't until my last breath I cried for my sleeping baby girl that he snapped out of his manic rage and released his hands from my neck.

I grabbed my daughter and whatever I could and headed for my 1997 Lexus. God was with me that night because everything that was wrong with the car disappeared. A car that never starts on the first or third try, kicked into high gear and took off faster than a dog chasing a cat.

Despite the thick ice on the ground that night, I drove off to Brooklyn, New York. There I was on familiar ground. The angels kept my daughter sleeping the entire time.

I drove to a vacant lot across the street from my friend's apartment and we slept in my car for six hours. Well, my daughter slept. My unrest wouldn't allow me to close my eyes. I drowned the heavens with thanks to the Lord for his protection. My daughter woke up at her usual time full of questions as to why we were in the car. It wasn't something I was ready to talk to her about. I just told her I would explain later.

When I finally got my composure back, I realized we could go to my sister's at least to bathe and refresh ourselves. The best cleansing I received was when I opened up to my sister and told her everything.

My sister had a one bedroom apartment. She gave up her bed to me and my youngest daughter while she slept on the couch. Living at my sister's place was the quickest place I could think of that wouldn't put my daughter and me out of routine in a short period of time.

Walking to the top of the Statue of Liberty felt shorter than the walk up the stairs to my sister's apartment. The bear hug we received was a confirmation she heard and understood everything I explained to her. She waited all her life to play the role of big sister and now here it was - my big sister was able to fulfill her dreams at this moment. She welcomed her niece and me into her home, as well as her heart.

The Lord found favor on me in so many ways I began to wonder why I didn't do this from the start. The elementary school that my daughter attended was within walking distance. The walk gave us time to talk and bond with each other more than driving in the car where I had to be focused on the road with other drivers. We walked to school every day with the assurance and confidence that things will get better for us.

My sister's neighborhood was miles away from my ex's house. We were far enough away where I could park and not be seen by him. I spent days in total euphoria since escaping from the torment and abuse of three years. I started to de-stress and cleanse my mind of the toxins he mentally instilled over those years. The distance did my daughter and I well, but despite the feeling of freedom, he was still able to track me down.

Never did I think he would arrive at my daughter's school and wait outside for me. The hardest thing for me was to remain calm and act as if nothing happened between him and me within the past four months.

Refusing to let him break me again, I proceeded to walk into the building without the acknowledgement of him sharing the same oxygen as me.

As he followed me and the crowd of children diminished into the building, I saw what appeared to be my guardian angel. The guy, who was the best man in my wedding, just happened to be the security guard on duty that morning. He saw the distress on my face.

A barrier between my abuser and I was created when he broke the distance. Terror filled my lungs as my abuser attempted to push past my friend. Wind blew past me as another security guard saw this and immediately jumped in to help him.

Police were called on my abuser (how ironic, a cop being called for a cop). The school lit up like the fourth of July as cop cars arrived. A colleague of my abuser escorted him off and the two security guards alerted the school not to allow him on the premises. In my hurry to leave, I did not think of a restraining order or order of protection against my abuser.

If you are going to live within the same town or nearby area, an order of protection for you and your children should also be in the plan.

**Contact your local police office to fill out the proper forms and find more information on the rights you have as a victim of abuse.

**Abuse is never okay. Contact the Domestic Abuse Hotline for help. 1-800- 789-SAFE (7233)

Seeking Refuge

The refuge at my sister's place only lasted three months. The person she was dealing with at the time was being released from prison and needed a place to stay, so my sister said we had to leave. By this point I was so used to being let down and disappointed, her asking us to leave hadn't even hurt me as much as it could have. While I didn't have much, I was however, able to acquire an apartment from the old landlord that originally rented an apartment to my ex-husband and me. The apartment was not ideal, but it was all I could afford at the time.

When I moved into the small one bedroom, I had no furniture and no money to buy any. The rent was $900 a month. I was making $1200 at my part time job. My car had so many tickets on it, that it was towed away and sold at an auction. I had to make up the difference between rent, other utilities, childcare and groceries, so I contacted some of my old hair clients and offered to service them in their homes. I had to carry all of my hair equipment and my six year old daughter on public transportation across town just to acquire enough money to make up for my rent and have money for groceries. I had no extra money for cable, so my daughter re-watched all of the videos she loved so much. At that point, she hadn't asked many questions about our situation, and I was grateful because I didn't have any real answers.

By now, I'm in the midst of phase two of my 180 Experience: Assessing. I had to pay $100 a month in child support that my oldest daughter's father demanded I pay through the courts. I had no car and nothing in my name, but I did have one thing going for me: I had a job. I felt confident that eventually my finances would get better.

When you assess your need for change, it often requires assessing your wrong doings. Acknowledging your wrongs is hardly ever easy. However, you'd be surprised at how much lighter you'll feel once you do it.

Admitting and Assessing will help you attain your "second chance" in all areas of your life.

Evaluate Your Thinking

As I continued the phase of Assessing, I began to eliminate the waste. Everything and everyone that served me no good purpose was eradicated. It was difficult for me to tell people (whether it be verbally or demonstrated through behavior) that I could no longer allow them to be a part of my life.

I had to destroy the toxins that were destroying me. I had to learn how to master changing the way I thought, and especially the way I was speaking about and to myself. My thoughts and words to myself were destructive. I was tearing my own self down.

Bit by bit I was breaking myself down in order to build myself up. I stopped interacting with people who did not have my best interest at heart. I didn't feel I had warriors who would go to battle with me and for me. It often times left me feeling unable to warrior for myself.

Admitting, Assessing, and Addressing can be a lonely road. You have to be your own hero. If you can get support from outside sources, than do so. Be sure that the help is authentic and only focuses on your healing, your growth and your transformation.

Change requires courage. It requires dedication. It requires knowing that there is a blessing on the other side of your pain.

The process of learning how to change your thinking takes time and tenacity. You have to allow yourself time to get into the groove of thinking positive, healthy thoughts that promote your overall wellness. I was never taught this growing up. I was always told I would be nothing. I heard this so many times that I clearly believed it.

I know that most of us do not claim the greatness we deserve in our lives. It is attached to our fear of success and failure. Success comes with a level of responsibility for more success. Failure comes with the accountability of starting over or giving up. Either way there is an outcome made up of our choices.

Tenacity is defined as a mandatory component when it comes to changing your thinking. It will not happen overnight. Please understand that if you've lived your lifetime thinking in a way that was not imparting a positive sense of self, it will take hard work and dedication to change toward positive thinking. Telling yourself thoughts, words, and ideas that infuse light and will promote your physical, emotional and mental well-being is key. Studies have shown it takes thirty consistent days of repeating positive words about yourself to yourself before you start to believe it and put it into action.

My pastor A. R. Bernard of Christian Cultural Center in Brooklyn, New York, taught me that change is not an event, it is a process. This simply means that the change you want and need to make, will require that you be tenacious. It will require you to consistently move toward the change you desire for your life.

Remember when you were in grade school and your teacher would go over a lesson plan multiple times? That was a part of your learning experience. You had to let what was being taught, sink in. Repetition is how we learn to retain information. I still remember moments and ideas that impacted me throughout my learning years. In elementary school, it was my first grade teacher Mrs. Safer. She was teaching us a song in French Frere Jacques. It's a basic repetitive tune. I haven't forgotten that and I'm 40+.

Breaking the Cycle

As a teenager, my mother dealt with her own demons of drug addiction and mental illness. She would persistently tell me that I never would amount to anything. She called me a bitch, a slut, beat me and told me that I wasn't worth anything. She never said I was good enough. Good grades needed to be better. No boyfriends. No sex. No talk about the "birds and the bees". I had no self-identity. I was insecure and knew nothing about my body, sex, or love. I watched her be in one abusive relationship after the other. The abuse came in different forms. Some were physical. Others were sexual. Some encouraged her substance abuse by supplying her with drugs. I learned nothing about self-love, feeling worthy or how to love myself.

Once I got from under her abuse, I repeated her mistakes. I didn't know what a healthy relationship looked like. I desired love, but had no representation of what love really was. My relationships were mostly sexual abuse. I was raped at thirteen, used by men twice my age for sex, and had one failed relationship after another. What did I learn? I learned that I was the problem just like my mother said. But one day, I had the revelation that I couldn't suffer in that pain anymore. Hence my 180 Experience.

Deep inside I knew that somehow, I was better than and more than what I was told. If you're hearing words that are breaking you down, DON'T BELIEVE THE LIES! You are good enough. You are loveable. You are worthy of love and happiness. You are equipped to conquer your fears. You can overcome the tragedies that you have experienced. There is nothing you can't do.

Keep in mind a 180 Experience can happen once or multiple times in your life. There is nothing wrong with re-inventing yourself multiple times. Look at some of the most successful people and you will see that they met many failures before their one success.

The Process

In order to reprogram your mind, you will have to train yourself to think differently. The way we think has an impact on how we address our lives. Your thoughts create an atmosphere for positive or negative results. You can't expect to have a loving, compassionate, loyal spouse if you are constantly telling yourself that you will never find that. If you think positive thoughts and you speak positive words, then the likelihood of having a positive outcome will be prevalent.

Most people grow comfortable with thinking negatively or having thoughts that are contrary to the results they want to have. You have to come to a place where you're just being honest with yourself. You cannot make the 180 in your life without being honest and open.

Training your mind to do a 180 away from the thoughts that have not served you well, is possible as long as you are consistent and persistent. It is possible to do a 180 at any age or stage in your life. You may be saying you are too old, or maybe you feel like you are too stuck in your ways. Maybe you feel like the power of positive thinking is bull. I can tell you from my own personal experience that you are so wrong. If you want to change how you think, you can absolutely do it.

As I reflect on the past, I can pinpoint every moment I've had to encourage myself not to go back to thinking I was less than enough. Making a 180 is a recurring process. I knew God called me to create *My Complete 180* because He knew He could use me to motivate and encourage others to make the same turn around I did.

During the shift to completing all three of the steps I've developed, it is imperative to not be critical of yourself. It has worked in my life, as well as for many other people that I have shared this with. Once you've admitted there needs to be change, you open up the door of opportunity to live a more fulfilled life. You can come up with a thousand different reasons why you can't, or just won't admit change needs to happen. You are only robbing yourself of a destiny of freedom.

Take Stock

You must assess your life. Assessing your life means to look at the core of who you are, where you have been, and where you need to go.

It means the ability to see your life as though you are outside looking in. Effectively you are taking a look at how to evaluate your own life and where you need to go from your current stage and onward. Notice I said current stage. The past already happened and although you can learn from it, you must not dwell on it.

Prioritize what is the most important thing you need to address first.

Alert yourself of hurt feelings or instances you did not let go of yet. It may be your current situation that is affecting you, and you need to pinpoint exactly what it is that is stirring up strife.

Assessing Will Help You Avoid Pitfalls

The biggest step in the program is Assessing. This is the place where you plot and plan. I'm sure you heard the cliché if you don't have a plan, you plan to fail. There will be so many thoughts going on in your head once you admit to the problem. These are a few questions you should ask yourself:

- "Where should I go?"
- "What should I do?"
- "Whom should I call?"
- "Do I flee or confront?"
- "What are my support systems?"
- "Do I have any money saved?"
- "Do I have a new job set up?"
- "Who can I trust to assist me?"
- "Am I able to move?"
- "Am I really serious about leaving this unhealthy relationship?"

YOU NEED A PLAN

It is always easier to say we are going to do something, versus actually doing it. That is not a plan.

One day at work my abuser called me multiple times and I refused every call. One of my co-workers, who was also an acquaintance, told my supervisor. She confronted me and asked me what was going on. As much as I didn't want to tell her, I knew then that this was my opportunity to start changing the dynamic of my future. Telling her my truth became a strategy. I told her that I was in an abusive relationship and that my abuser was stalking me. I knew that it was time for me to make a plan to get away from my ex for good.

The first part of my plan involved changing my cell phone number. Since my abuser didn't have that connection to me anymore, he had to resort to stalking me on my job. He followed me to work and used his police connections to find out the number to my job location. This scared me, and it unnerved my supervisor. She told me that for my safety and for the safety of all staff, she needed to change my work location. The next day I was in a different location.

At this point, I decided to apply for a promotion. About two months later, I got the promotion and moved to another location. I would change my route to work daily. I looked over my shoulder all of the time. I was afraid, but I knew that I had to move forward. While at my new position in a new location, guess what? He found me and started calling me all over again. So I knew then, I had to get confrontational. I would tell him to stop calling every time he did, and I remained steadfast in not going back out of fear or comfortability.

During this time, I began my journaling. I wrote everything down. My feelings, fears, ideas, motivations, plans, revised plans, contacts that would benefit me sooner or later, goals and when I planned on accomplishing them. I took my journal everywhere and slept with it on my nightstand with a pen ready to jot down prayers, thoughts and plans, because I knew I would inevitably wake up in the middle of the night. I left no stone unturned. I answered the questions we previously discussed. I knew I couldn't stay at this job too much longer, so I began applying for other ones. However, a great opportunity came up at my current job and I decided to take it. It involved me returning to school to get my master's degree in Social Work. I also decided to change my conversations with myself. I told myself that my abuser no longer had power over me. I was taking that power back!

You too can take your power back. Plot and plan before you do anything else. You will succeed at making the changes you desire to make. You will have the 180 Experience you desire.

The Exit Strategy

When I got to the point that I was ready to break away from the abusive relationship that I was in, I needed to have an exit strategy. Having an exit strategy for an abusive relationship often times means life or death. As a therapist, I learned early on to never tell a woman who was in an abusive relationship to just leave. Without a plan, it is usually when the abuse intensifies or even death of the victim can occur.

When you make an exit strategy from your abuser, include time frames, support systems, where your financial backing is coming from (have no less than three to six months of savings tucked away if at all possible), find one person you trust who knows you're exiting the relationship in case things get escalated, they will know your plan and can relay that to authorities if need be, secure new housing so that your abuser won't be able to locate you, seek counseling to help you recover from this traumatic event. These are a few things to think over before you take that step away from your abuser:

- Who is going to be helping you? You cannot do it all alone. Find someone (or people) you know you can trust.
- How soon will you be ready to make your personal changes?
- How do you plan to maintain the changes you intend to make?
- If you have children, have you secured daycare or schooling for them when you move?
- Have you considered counseling or joining a support group to help you along your journey to your 180?

Once these steps have been taken you are ready to move on.

BREATHE

Assessing a situation is like having a bird's eye view of your life.

We all can benefit from putting our needs before anyone else's. Why do you think when we fly, we are instructed to place oxygen on us first, before others? Simply put, we cannot provide others with what we deny to ourselves. If you deny yourself love, you cannot love.

Commitment to being at your best in order to divide pieces of yourself to those around you means you first must be giving yourself what you need. If you can't breathe on the plane, how do you expect the person next to you to survive? We can become exhausted constantly giving away ourselves and never refueling. If we run out of gas in our cars, we take the time to gas up so we can get to where we need to go. The same must be applied to us. Gas up!

Some of us are helping others with their life support when we are the ones who need the support. It's not about being selfish, it's about advocating self-first. Self-care is important. You can become mentally and physically depleted constantly giving and never receiving. You can cause yourself physical harm by not putting yourself first. That is why so many of us have strokes, heart attacks and other ailments. Our lives are busy in today's world, but my theory is that sometimes all you need is a "five." Five minutes to just breathe and rid yourself of some of life's stressors. The time you spend stuck in traffic you can use as a time to pray, reflect on what you need to do for the day or on how well your day went - versus cursing and complaining that you're sitting in a parking lot on the highway. Our mental well-being depends on thinking more positively.

DEEP BREATHS

Breathing helps clear your mind and you will be able to focus and concentrate on the main issue that you need to clarify and move on with.

As you breathe, do not just breathe in a way that is normal or in a way where you find yourself hyperventilating. You want each breath to count as a moment and time for you to meditate and relax. This is where mindfulness comes into play.

The way you want to breathe is as if you were visiting your doctor for your annual checkup. You know the way they tell you to breathe in, then breathe out? You want to follow the same procedure.

Start with an inhale from deep within. This is a way of taking in all the oxygen that you can hold inside of you.

Do not take in too much air where you will find yourself losing your breath, but rather take in as much air as you think you can. Hold it in you for about three seconds, then release.

During these three seconds clear your mind of nonessential things. Do not think about:

- What you have to do
- What to do next
- Where you left your keys
- Or who's on Facebook

Rather focus on the breath itself and separating yourself from everything that serves you no good.

You want to exhale slowly. Do not just push it out. Do not try to make it as if you are exercising and have to go to the next thing. Let it slowly move out like a soft wave in the ocean. You want to do this five times helping you to release negative energy. You want to be in a state of mindfulness.

According to Merriam-Webster, mindfulness is a state of heightened or complete awareness of one's thoughts, emotions, or experiences.

As you are breathing, you want to release all the stress and tension starting from the bottom of your feet all the way to your head. The way to do this is to tap into yourself being a full vessel and you want the particles and bad energy to evaporate. As you exhale, you are releasing that into the atmosphere and out of the vessel, which is your body. Again as you inhale lift all that energy, tension, stress, and aggravation from your toes and exhale it out into the atmosphere. As you exhale out, say to yourself and repeat this: "I release you. I release you. I release you." This will help you also focus and feel like you are getting rid of whatever it is that is weighing you down. You want to do this and repeat it all the way until you feel you have extracted all tension, stress, anger and animosity out of your body. Once everything is clear from your body and mind you are ready for the next step.

In as much as my abuser controlled every aspect of my life, I still existed somewhere deep inside. Although I was losing pieces of myself daily, there was still the version of me that God created. I had to hold on to the idea that God loves me and that the story of my life was not going to end at this pinnacle moment. Something inside of me knew that my journey hadn't ended. There were many more chapters ahead for me.

Part 3

Address

Admitting to yourself in an honest and realistic way, and gathering all the information you've collected during the assess phase is great, but until you address the problem things will stay the same. Addressing the situation is the last and most vital step.

The attempt I took on my own life heightened my awareness that I needed to address my relationship situation and more importantly, look at my own reflection in the mirror. I had to address that I was scared, felt powerless, and realized I didn't belong in the place that ultimately felt like a tunnel I couldn't climb out of.

Only I could recognize what I needed to do in order to better help myself. The same goes for you. The mistakes we make in our lives prepare us for what's ahead. Nothing that occurs in your life is wasted.

While I was in that toxic relationship, I couldn't see the purpose for everything I had experienced in that three year period. It took me years to cleanse and renew myself. It all happened by creating, and initially taking, the three steps of the 180 system.

The next phase that I will walk you through is how to address your situation so that you can take the final step in your 180 Experience.

There are three keys to unlocking this phase: Write, Reflect, & Visualize. This process I developed has been working for me, friends, family, and many of the clients that I counsel – and it will work for you, too. So let's get started!

Write to Heal

Once I was able to admit to myself I was in an abusive relationship and realized my priority, I was able to breathe. Being at my sister's house also gave me the opportunity to not only think about what I went through, but to realize it is best to write it down as proof of the abuse. It also helped me to visually see what I needed to do next in terms of moving forward.

The best thing I did for myself was write in a journal. Having a journal helped me keep stock of what was happening in my life.

Inside this journal was everything that was happening to me. I also wrote how I felt each day. Never did I think I would look back on it and say "Wow! Look at what I went through. Look at what I overcame."

I was able to see where I grew, areas where I was abused and taken advantage of, and didn't know it. The great thing about having a journal is you can let it go. Get everything off your chest.

Don't worry about what you should write or how. Don't even worry about the grammar, or if what you are saying makes sense. Journaling is not about getting it right or being perfect so if your sentence structure, or penmanship isn't correct, **DON'T WORRY!**

Some people draw pictures or stencil art in their journal. They did it either for fun or a way to visualize what they wrote. Whatever you decide: just write!

Once you get to a place where you've poured out all of your emotions in your journal, take time to go back and assess your situation. This will help you immediately notice the areas where you need to work on. I recommend doing this step on a weekly basis.

Had I taken a look at my journal on a weekly basis to assess it, some of my issues could have been avoided sooner. However, I do understand that everything happens in its own time. I say that because even if I looked back at my journal during the time of my abuse, I probably would have made up an excuse about the treatment I was receiving and avoided trying to rectify it.

We all need time to reflect on our day and see areas that we could have made different decisions, and journaling will help with this.

Writing everything that is consuming us can be a bit overwhelming. However, writing the things that are at the forefront will be a great place to start. Visually seeing things can oftentimes make a big difference in revealing what is really a priority to you. Write it all down and simplify it. You want to set achievable goals for yourself. Journaling is an excellent tool to help you organize your action plan. This step can be tedious. Though, it will be worth the work you will put into it.

Goal setting is about assessing where you are and what you need to do to get to the next step. With writing down your goals, there needs to be the consideration of an amount of reasonable progress in a measurable amount of time. Remember -- it is a process. If the plan does not work, change the plan, but not the goal. Don't shelf these things.

There are two things to keep in mind when setting goals: 1) Write down a collection of ways you are great. 2) List how you overcame circumstances. Do not look at how the abuser insulted you or degraded your value. We have to first remove self-scrutiny from the equation. Putting yourself down slows the process of a 180 Experience from occurring. It is like having dead weight carried on your back. Use this step to release the heaviness that you've been carrying around in your spirit.

Verbal Abuse is Abuse!

Verbal abuse is something overlooked. Whoever said sticks and stones may break my bones but words will never hurt me, obviously never had a bad word said about or to them. If they did, it must have been from people they didn't care about in the first place.

When my abuser wasn't physically hurting me, he sure knew how to smack me around with some toxic words. Dumb, stupid, can't do anything right, you talk too much, you're frustrating me, no one really loves you; these are words if said enough times can change the image you have of yourself. It will tear you down. When you are addressing, you must never say negative things about where you were, who you are, and especially where you are going. Verbal abuse towards yourself needs to cease as well. Start speaking life into yourself.

Reflection is Key

When assessing my life, I noticed I didn't have a positive reflection of myself. I was so used to hearing things like, "You're so stupid", "You are nothing", "You're such an idiot" that these terms became a part of who I thought I was. Be very careful not to say these types of things to yourself. These negative words are not going to improve you.

It's very important that you speak positively about yourself. Look in the mirror and say out loud:

- "I HAVE IMPROVED!"
- "I LOVE MYSELF!"
- "I AM POWERFUL, SUCCESSFUL, LOVEABLE AND A MAGNET FOR POSITIVITY!"

Repeat these or others you come up with twice a day for a month. Eventually this will be your life mantra. Positive affirmations should be a part of your daily routine. Not only should you affirm yourself, but also affirm all that you seek to obtain in life.

If you repeat something consistently, it eventually becomes what you believe. The human mind then starts acting on it. You will not only believe what you say, but you will do whatever is necessary to make it true. One of the best ways to help you remember you are on the way to improvement is to visualize your plan of action.

Ways to Visualize

As we book lovers know, reading the book is always better than seeing it in the movies, but don't we all say after reading a book, "Man, I hope this would be made into a movie." The same is true for our 180 process. We can write down our goals and plan of action all we want, but until we can see ourselves free of the bondage we're in, those plans do not go into effect and the impact just isn't there.

In this part of addressing you want to ask yourself a few questions. (Make sure to write these in your journal).

- How do I feel about my current well-being?
- Have I tried to change my current status?
- If yes, how did I try to work it out? Can this method work someplace else in my life?
- When I changed my circumstance, what happened?
- What is the one thing I really need to focus on now?
- Did I seek help?

There are different types of help and depending on the severity of the situation you're in matters when you seek help from outside.

I sought my sister. I also had to remove myself from the situation quickly. I was blessed enough to have a family member I could go to. I didn't know if she would be willing to take in my daughter and me, but I was thankful she did.

We may not be that fortunate at all times. This is why while assessing it is important you ask yourself: **do I have an escape haven?**

Most of the time we are so focused on getting out that we do not even think about where we are going. We are so excited about discovering we can be free, that we forget to plan how to get free.

Without a plan, you plan to fail.

Plan Your Escape

Your safe haven has to be a place of tranquility. It cannot be in an environment where you are going to feel more stressed or scared. Make sure it is a place where time is not a restriction so you can heal and come to a full 180 before moving on. Time only heals wounds if you are **WORKING** on healing yourself from them.

Your new home should have a reflection of you. Again, this can be applied to any situation in your life; your new work "home", your new relationship "home", your new physical appearance "home". Let everything around you be a reflection of your best you.

If this is a situation of abuse, make sure your safe haven is in a secure area where the abuser does not have easy access to you. List a few places where you know you can go to in case you have to flee. Here are a few things you should have on hand just in case:

Name of Place

Address of Place

Main Number

Contact Person

Contact Number

Contact Email

School & Address

Nearby Facilities

Who resides there?

How long can you stay?

How far is it from the abuser?

Are the premises secured?

How many exits are in the building?

Despite the trauma, the heartache, and the abuse -- everything brought me to where and who I am today.

When programmers find a glitch in their program, they trace back through their notes to see where they possibly coded incorrectly. This should be the same for your life. You want to go back to when it all started, no matter how painful it might be. Starting from the beginning and moving forward will help you visualize the scenarios it took to get you where you are now.

If you're one of those people who asks themselves, "How did I get into this mess?" You will see how starting from the beginning will answer your question.

My life went through its obstacles. I was able to escape my abuser, but not without making drastic decisions in my life.

The plan doesn't work if you don't work it. You must be willing to say to yourself, that there is a way to improve your life. You just have to map out how. You want to go about it in a methodical way. "Procrastination is a thief." Waiting too long to complete or even create a goal will rob you. Opportunities do not come knocking at our door. We need to create our own opportunities for change.

Questions for Thought

The 180 process can be used for anything in your life. It is best when you feel something went off track in your life to use this process.

When going through your 180, it always seems like everything is a priority to resolve. The best way to narrow it down is to build your questions like an upside down pyramid.

Start with the big issue first. Continue with what led to that issue, then the next issue, and so forth. Your life will begin to unfold as if an onion is being peeled. When you get to the root of the matter, you will see that small issue grew into something so big all around it.

What is the issue most concerning me?

_____

_____

_____

_____

_____

_____

What is the result of my life currently because of this issue?

_____

_____

_____

_____

_____

_____

_____

Did anyone contribute to this issue? Or is this something I have not dealt with of my own doing?

_____

_____

_____

_____

_____

Is anyone helping me through this?

_____

_____

_____

_____

_____

How could I have initiated a different outcome?

_____

_____

_____

_____

_____

Is anyone else affected by my current issue?

_____

_____

_____

_____

_____

If anyone else is being affected by my issue, who?
How does this make me feel?

_____

_____

_____

_____

_____

What can I do to prevent this from continuing? (List more than one way of prevention)

_____

_____

_____

_____

_____

_____

_____

_____

_____

What were the signs leading up to the issue that I currently deal with?

_____

_____

_____

_____

_____

What can I do differently?

_____

_____

_____

_____

How will this help me in the future?

_____

_____

_____

_____

_____

What was the root issue?

_____

_____

_____

_____

_____

Can I avoid this from recurring?

_____

_____

_____

_____

_____

Is there anyone I have to confront about my issue?

_____
_____
_____
_____
_____

What will be my approach to handling the situation?

_____
_____
_____
_____
_____
_____
_____

CONCLUSION

Summing It All Up

So Where am I Now?

Having all that I assessed, I knew it would take my strength, my courage, and my confidence to live a fulfilled life. The end of 2014 and mid-way into 2015 would shift and change my life forever. Life will bring things to your front door that you never ordered. I wanted to replace a return to sender stamp on the experiences I was about to encounter. I felt as though I had been through enough already in the past few years, now here comes even bigger battles for me to fight. Clearly God truly makes us soldiers because I was headed for war once again.

In December of 2014, I began to experience the worst pain I'd ever felt in the left side of my face. The pain was like an electrical shock-like, stabbing, burning pain. The pain existed in my lower jaw and nostril area mostly. However, the agonizing feeling was also present in my forehead and eye area.

After visiting my Primary Physician, Dentist, Ear Nose & Throat Doctor and a Neurologist, no one could explain why I was experiencing such excruciating pain. After adamantly Googling my symptoms over and over again, I visited another Neurologist who within five minutes of me explaining my symptoms, diagnosed me with Trigeminal Neuralgia. Trigeminal Neuralgia or TN is a brain/facial pain disorder that affects the fifth cranial nerve. An artery or arteries compress on the nerve and it creates this pain that is unbearable. The fifth cranial nerve located behind the ear is where sensory signals are sent to the forehead, cheek, jaw, and nostril. The pain is unforgiving and can make the strongest person want to throw in the towel.

After months of being on anticonvulsant medication, the doctor told me I would have to have a Craniotomy. That's right, Brain Surgery. I would need someone to help care for me twenty-four-seven thereafter. I gave my independence a hug and waved it goodbye for a season. This was the hardest decision for me after newly regaining my independence. I needed to have Brain Surgery to reduce the compression which was supposed to reduce the amount of pain I was feeling.

The surgery was not a success. I experienced reduced pain for two months after the surgery, but due to astronomical stress, I didn't properly heal. Not quite healed and unable to work, I moved to another state to begin a new life. This move was already in the works before I even knew I needed the surgery. So I committed to the move.

Unfortunately in 2017, I had to endure a second Brain Surgery to further alleviate the pressure on my brain from more compressed arteries that are a result of the Trigeminal Neuralgia. It took months for me to recover. I was bedridden for four months and then when I was able to walk, I needed a walker. I was and still am frustrated that I have to live with this disorder, but I still smile my way through every day, focusing on helping others live their lives fulfilled and purposeful. I still deal with many side effects, like loss of memory, pain, vision and hearing difficulties, imbalance, and the need to be on medication indefinitely. But, I'm still standing!

I work on making a 180 daily; training my mind to admit I have some limitations, assessing the ways I can work within the idea of my new standard of living and address my life, goals, parenting, love, business, etc. in a way that is empowering, encouraging and inspiring.

I now live a successful, prosperous life. I am so laser focused on maintaining my health, being there for my family, ensuring I am always making myself a priority, and building my business to impact the lives of those around me. I not only survived, but thrived in spite of the TN and the life challenges I've faced.

AND YOU CAN TOO!

If you change your thinking, you can transform the way you live. That is the 180 mission. The three step process can be applied to just about any aspect of your life. Just remember, follow the process all the way through.

Questions for Thought

What are the main issues concerning me right now?

_____

_____

_____

_____

_____

_____

_____

Did I meet the issue head on?

_____

_____

_____

_____

Did I effectively communicate my exact issue?

_____

_____

_____

_____

Did I approach my situation with assurance and authority?

_____

_____

_____

_____

_____

What are my future goals? How will I accomplish them? What will be the timeframe do so?

_____

_____

_____

_____

_____

_____

_____

_____

How will I sustain my changes and growth?

_____

_____

_____

_____

_____

What self-care measures do I have in place?

_____

_____

_____

_____

_____

How will I avoid future pitfalls of bad relationships?

_____

_____

_____

_____

_____

How will I affirm my love for myself?

_____

_____

_____

_____

_____

Notes

Notes

Notes

Notes

Notes

Acknowledgements

Thank you God for revelation, love, wisdom and salvation. I could not have done anything without you. My daughters Cheyenne and Nyesa, mommy loves you in everlasting ways. Thank you for the opportunity to be steward over your lives. Thank you for your love, passion to see me win, laughter, tears, healing and closeness we have.

To my grandsons, Big Sisters Toni & Dina, Boo Thang; Arlise, Joy, Nicole, Kay Belle, Astrid, Cindy, Fritz; my brothers, nephews, niece, grand-nephews, mom, all of my prayer warriors, family, supporters, and tribe. I love y'all.

Thank you to everyone who dedicated their time in bringing this book into fruition.

About the Author

A. Marie Davis is a Licensed Social Worker and Transformational Mindset Coach who has been impacting lives for close to 20 years. She started her business from the ground up. Literally! After surviving abuse of all kinds in a long-term relationship and losing everything because of it, God used that experience along with her passion for changing the lives of others to create her Life Enhancement and Personal Transformation business -- *My Complete 180*.

Using her creative talents, educational background and life experiences, A. Marie has nurtured *My Complete 180* into a powerful resource to help other women navigate through the struggles and obstacles they face in their everyday lives. She empowers them to create life changing goals and gives them the tools they need to obtain sustainable change. That is the mission of *My Complete 180*. Her clients have found that by working corporately with A. Marie their lives have been completely overhauled. They have seen the difference how shifting their mindsets has positively impacted their lives. Mindfulness is everything!

A. Marie hopes that through taking her journey with her in this book, you'll quickly see how possible it is to transform your own life if you just Admit, Assess, Address, repeat.

Affiliations

Jessica LeAnn is an author, brand strategist, editor and literary coach. She has written books for black teen girls as well as aspiring authors. She has over 10 years of experience in self-publishing. Jessica teaches authors how to build their brands, write, publish and successfully sell their books.

jessica@chocolatereadings.com

www.chocolatereadings.com

Made in the USA
San Bernardino, CA
16 July 2019